On the
Crossroads of
Asia and Europe

Poems of Tomasz Jastrun

Translated from the Polish by

Daniel Bourne

SALMON RUN PRESS
Anchorage, Alaska

On the Crossroads
of Asia and Europe

ISBN 1-887573-05-4

Salmon Run Press
P. O. Box 672130
Chugiak, AK 99567-2130

Printed in the United States of America

Contents

A Time for Remembrance and Forgetting

Prose (1989-1997)

Translator's Introduction

Let's start with a poem of Tomasz Jastrun, "A Secret Meeting," a piece that seems simple enough, at least in the first few lines, but by the end leads us into a world that is certainly not one of birthday candles and cake, but the absurdities inherent in early 1980s Poland, a country that had started the decade off with hope in the form of the Solidarity Free Trade Movement, but now in 1982 was facing the destruction of this dream:

> He tells me there will be cake
> With seven candles
> Which he will blow out
> His cheeks puffed up
> With the whole world inside
> And only when leaving he requests
> *Don't come home then*
> *You know they know*
> *When I was born*
>
> I heard afterwards
> That no one came
> To get me
> Meanwhile the birthday was a success
> The children played
> Internment camp
> And to finish
> Stood the youngest up and shot him

In the space of 17 lines of poetry, we've made a journey into the heart of Poland's martial law period—as well as Tomasz Jastrun's experience within it. On December 13, 1981, Poland awoke to a Sunday morning that featured not only the first heavy snow of the winter season, but tanks on the streets and special riot troops poised to take action. During the night, martial law had been declared by a self-proclaimed Military Council for National Salvation, headed by General Wojciech Jaruzelski. Solidarity activists—both intellectuals and workers—were rounded up and put into internment camps. The nation's media, which had begun to open up during the Solidarity period, was brought back under strict control. (Even the evening news anchorman appeared in military uniform.) Nightly curfews and travel restrictions were imposed, as was the censorship of mail and telephone calls.

But there were interesting public relations twists as well. To show their integrity, the authorities would stamp all letters as being censored rather than censor them on the sly. When you picked up the telephone to call someone, rather than a dial tone there would be a voice repeating over and over that your call was being monitored. On the streets of Poland appeared a remarkable propaganda poster, showing a little girl pointing upwards to a map of Poland, outlined in what seemed to be dark-red crayon. The caption at the bottom read: *We have only one Poland.* It was a message that seemed to argue not only that there could only be one authority in Poland, but also that Poland did not have multiple lives, that Poland had needed to be invaded by itself in order to keep the Soviets from coming in and completely devastating the country. Meanwhile, the authorities even published a book presenting their case for the imposition of martial law (available in bookstores throughout the country despite a general dearth of books or magazines), which took as its epigraph not a quotation from Marx or Lenin, but from an obscure Renaissance political thinker with overtones of Machiavelli—Juan Alfonso Lancina: "The first right of every state is to watch out for its own existence."

*   *   *   *

Born in 1950, Tomasz Jastrun by the beginning of martial law had already published his poetry widely in both official and unofficial presses, including his early collections *Bez usprawiedliwienia* (*Without Justification,* 1978) and *Promienie blednego kola* (*Pulsations from a Vicious Circle*), for which he received the Polish PEN Club's 1981 Robert Graves Award for Poetry.

Then, during 1980-81, he became active as an editor for a Solidarity cultural journal, as a result ending up on the list of individuals to be detained on the night of December 13. However, when the police came for him, he was not at home. Rather than turn himself in, he chose to go into hiding, where he remained until arrested in October 1982. Afterwards, he was interned at Bialoleka Prison until released under a general amnesty on December 23, 1982. While still in hiding, Jastrun wrote the poems for his first underground book of poetry, *Na skrzyzowaniu Azji i Europy* (*On the Crossroads of Asia and Europe*), printed in the summer of 1982. Also, his stay at Bialoleka occasioned the poems for a second unofficially-printed book, *Biala laka, dziennik poetycki* (*The White Meadow Prison Diary*), which appeared in the summer of 1983.

Collectively, these two books create a powerful window on a very turbulent period. But, this poetry is not mere documentation with line-breaks; rather, it is a poetry that re-sees this history through Jastrun's iconic yet iconoclastic lens—a filter that often accomplishes being reverential and ironic at the same time. Indeed, along with his imprisonment at Bialoleka, Jastrun's experience in being on the lam for several months—a period in which he was basically free to travel anywhere in the country except to his own home because that was the one place the authorities expected him to go—put him in a position from which to endure martial law as both prisoner and fugitive. However, it's not just a matter of Jastrun having powerful experiences as the late 20th Century Underground Man. Rather, it's the way he connects the personal with the political, the intimate with the national, that makes his work resonate. Taking such elemental images as the sanctity (or violation) of the home, or awkward night-time discussions between father and son about good and evil, he is able to portray the surrounding tragedy affecting not just Poland in the 1980s, but other times and places as well—Bosnia, East Timor, Burma, Kosovo—when people are weighted down by brute force or media corruption. Furthermore, Jastrun is not afraid to re-evaluate and criticize the national mythos that his poetry deals with so frequently. Although his poetry is heavily dependent on allusions to recent and not-so-recent Polish history, his perspective is also frequently sardonic, something that lands him in hot water to this day. Indeed, it is one thing to decry the pervasiveness of media and cultural corruption in his martial law-era poem "Beasts:"

They say our Madonna in Zyrardow
Has joined the party
They open her I.D.
To show the photo
And the two scars on her cheek

They say Christ in Bialoleka Prison
Signed an oath of loyalty
On TV they turn the camera
On a pale white sheet
With a red smudge

They say the twelve apostles petitioned
To dissolve Solidarity
Holed up in their office
They break out the mineral water
And only one is sad

Now there is ironclad proof
Even the cross won't deny the rights of state
Or that the Star of Bethlehem was red

While we the steadfast
Tough and disbelieving
Are thrown to the beasts
Of lies   betrayal   hypocrisy

But, Jastrun's tendency to question, to act as gadfly, has also extended into the post-Communist era, where his acerbic essays on Polish culture and society (often under the pseudonyms of Witold Charlamp and, more recently, Smecz--which in Polish means "slam") have won him awards and a wide readership, but also a fair measure of criticism. An example of this ongoing rapier wit occurs in his essay on the 1997 meeting of the two Polish Nobel Laureates for Poetry, Czeslaw Milosz and Wislawa Szymborska, in the Royal Castle in Warsaw:

> The Laureates appeared with an entourage—a much too numerous entourage—of photojournalists. A woman's choir dressed in green robes intoned a song in Latin. Meanwhile, the Laureates were positioned opposite two chairs and then offered as prey to the photographers. In the midst of the countless flashes, in the angelic singing, the two appeared to be heaven's elect. Szymborska was suffering, wishing she could dematerialize on the spot, while Milosz scowled with dignity. This scene lasted so frightfully long as to tax even the strongest constitution, but the Laureates survived this trial of the flash and, once more elevated on the wings of the choir, they neared the antique table swarming with microphones.

But one thing certain is that Jastrun has become a very prominent voice. Already in 1983 Jastrun received the cultural prize "S" from Underground Solidarity for his poetry during martial law. During the remainder of the 1980s, besides publishing award-winning essays in *Kultura* and *ResPublica,* and being a founding editor of the leading underground literary monthly *Wezwanie* from 1981-88, he also published several books of poetry, *Kropla kropla* (*Drop by Drop*, 1985), *Wezel polski* (*The Polish Knot*, 1988), and *Obok siebie* (*Beside Oneself*, 1989), all published officially, and *Czas pamieci i zapomnienia* (*A Time for Remembrance and Forgetting*, 1987), published in the underground press. (Indeed, throughout the 1980s, Jastrun published both above and below ground, frequently with the same poem appearing in both places). In 1985 Jastrun traveled to America on a Kosciuszko Foundation fellowship, where he gathered material for his book of essays on American and Polish American culture, *W zlotej klatce* (*In a Gilded Cage, 1986*). He also was a recipient of the Koscielski Prize in 1986, an award given in Geneva, Switzerland to outstanding younger Polish writers.

In the 1990s, his essays have included the series *Dziennik zewnetrzny* (*Exterior Journal*), published in *Kultura*, and *Z ukosa* (*Awry*; or, *From a Slant*, collected and published in 1992), while he has published several books of poetry, including two with the straightforward titles of *42 Wiersze* (*42 Poems*, 1995) and *Wiersze*

(*Poems*, 1997), as well as two bilingual collections in Germany and Sweden. From 1990 until 1994, Jastrun was the cultural ambassador to Sweden, after which he returned to Warsaw in order to concentrate more on his writing and to produce the television cultural program *Pegaz* (*Pegasus*) from 1992-1996. Currently he writes for a number of leading Polish journals and magazines.

* * * *

I first met Jastrun while I was in Poland on a exchange program from Indiana University to Warsaw University. It was during the winter of 1983, soon after Jastrun had been released from Bialoleka, and immediately after the death of his father, Mieczyslaw Jastrun, one of the most famous Polish poets in 20th century Poland, a connection that made Tomasz a high-profile target for the authorities (though it also afforded him, perhaps, some protection as well). During this first meeting, Jastrun still wore the beard he had grown to disguise himself while in hiding. He was very quiet. Around him, martial law was still going on, but it seemed to have entered another stage, one less virulent, but nonetheless exhausting. Throughout the rest of the 1980s, "official" Communist Poland and "unofficial" Poland (Solidarity, the black market, underground literary presses and other cultural forces) split further and further apart. Then, finally, the regime gave up the fight. In 1989 came the Round Table talks between the Jaruzelski government and Solidarity. Free elections were scheduled for that Fall, and the rest, as they say, is history.

Throughout my work with Jastrun since 1982, including on a Fulbright fellowship to Poland in 1985-87, I've been grateful for his willingness to talk through the various linguistic puzzles in his writing. He's been gracious, accommodating, witty, incisive. During the cultural limbo-land of the late 80s, he once bemoaned that not even political reform was enough, that "we are all children of the system," and unable to change. Later, in 1993, during the dog-eat-dog capitalism rampant in Poland during the early post-Communist era, I visited him in Stockholm before returning to Poland for my first visit since 1989. He summed up Poland this way: "The restaurants are improved, but the sidewalks are in worse shape than ever." On a more personal note, Jastrun once boasted that he was the best poet amongst all Polish tennis players--as well as the best tennis player of all Polish poets. . .

As a translator, I long ago learned that the hardest thing to translate is what occurs between the lines. By this I mean that it's the sounding board inside the reader in the original language that makes a poem work as much as it is the various linguistic choices of the poet (one of the reasons why Walt Whitman's comment that great poetry demands great readers makes so much sense). In the upcoming translations I try to handle that translation of cultural, historical, linguistic context as organically as possible. But, at times, I do resort to a footnote. But where do I stop, how far back do I go? One of the most compelling aspects of Polish literature is that it is a giant palimpsest—the present written on layers and layers of the past. And, when you start to dig down, you can very easily sink, never to come back up. So do I go back to World War II, the Nazi occupation, the first stirrings of 20th century underground culture in the form of secret universities and presses? To the partitions period between 1795 and the end of World War I, in which Poland was hacked up between Prussia, Austria and Russia—yet survived because of an enduring national consciousness based to a large degree on Polish literature? To the very first centuries of the Polish state and its grapplings with invasions from the West (the Teutonic Knights) and from the East (the Mongols). Indeed, Poland has been on the political and cultural fault lines between Europe and Asia, East and West, for a long, long time.

Wooster, Ohio, August 31, 1998

On the
Crossroads of
Asia and Europe

Afghanistan

On the soldiers' shoulders
Ride the white doves of peace
With their eyes poked out

As long as the Afghan people
Are in need of help
The soldiers will remain
And remain and remain

We cry out
Butterflies and crickets in bondage
But who will understand
The language of butterflies and crickets

Those breathing freedom
Have a different set of problems
A shorter memory
They slip off to sleep untroubled
One day to wake up
In Afghanistan

Sleeplessness

All night my son couldn't sleep
He lay with his eyes wide open
Without a sound
Until just before daybreak he told me
He was afraid of war
Of strangers
With their faces frozen on
Who would bust open the door
To our home

I try to soothe him
That life like a fairy tale
Has a happy ending
But he is too old for fairy tales
And looks at me with suspicion

I turn my eyes away because I know
That tomorrow they will come
They will come and tell us
That the devil does exist
They will come and tell us
That the world is a broken toy
No one can repair
They will come the more menacing
Because they themselves are miserable
With stars on their foreheads
Carved out of meat and bone

*The First Night**

In the middle of the night
A girl raced in
Like a flame
She swayed in the doorway
It's begun

Snow was falling
Flakes tightened into fists
The pavement glazed with ice
Joyous drunks
Staggered on the sidewalk

A friend's apartment already empty
Only the remembered shape of a man
Poised in the doorway
Absence stamped onto thin air

The doors of dawn
Busted with a crowbar
Already light
And there in a mirror
Rescued from disaster
I saw my own face
Frightening
Because it still looked the same

*On December 13, 1981, martial law was declared in Poland. During the
night, thousands of Solidarity activists throughout the country were rounded up
and interned.

Feathers

Tonight I banged at a lot of doors
Some barely hanging to their hinges
Emptied rooms where in vain
The mirrors kept from breaking
And the rugs bristled like dogs

But there were other homes as well
Where people stood in the doorway
And standing in their eyes
Fear and anger

And on this night everybody
Had run so far out of hope
That I decided—there was no other way—
I should wake up the Lord God himself
Only I found no door to pound on

But I saw he had left his window
Wide open dark
And through it the snow fell like feathers
From a pillow ripped open by a knife

Visitation

Four of them
In the middle of the night
One in uniform
One with crowbar
Two with smiles

Where's your husband
They raced off to check each room
Swished the drapes back and forth
Frosted the breath of our sleeping child
Then they each found a chair
To wait me out

Four angels of communism
In their mouths black tidings from on high

*Hands**

On the murdered miners in the earth
The hair and fingernails still lengthen

Their sun a lump of coal
Their road a black tunnel

Their bodies covered with sand
The lies
Packed in place by a policeman's boot

Yet on the murdered miners
The hair and fingernails still grow
And their wiry fingers
Towards the throats of those who pulled the trigger

*In late December 1981, days after the imposition of Polish martial law, an occupation strike in the "Wujek" coal mine in Silesia was broken by force. At least eight miners lost their lives in the defense of the mine, and many more were wounded.

10

To My Son

I picked him up
Pressed his warm cheek
To my own
This was our goodbye

Then for a long time
I felt in my breast
His small heart beat
As I skirted the dark walls
Of the military curfew
The walls on which someone had written
Down with Fascism—Solidarity Will Triumph

The soldiers on the crossroads
Of Asia and Europe
Warmed their red hands
Over coal blazing from a steel drum

Fear yanked on a man's collar
Who ran to the prison of his own home

The last bus tonight
Dragged in its wake
A net of stars

And among the night's catch of galaxies
I saw my son's future
Slung out on the only shore left

On the Crossroads

Soldiers strap on their machine gun crosses
They are given gall to numb their lips

No one will give them water
No one will give them food

And when somebody asks
Why have you come here
They stammer out their orders
And stammer out their fear

By twilight the fires will be lit
In their cast-iron drums
As they fend off the Polish night
The face of a dead brother

Mothers of soldiers grind on their hand-mills
Grating the hours and the shells of their rosaries
And when they pray they wring their hands
Over the empty bellies
That gave birth to Cain and Abel

A Secret Meeting

He tells me there will be cake
With seven candles
Which he will blow out
His cheeks puffed up
With the whole world inside
And only when leaving he requests
Don't come home then
You know they know
When I was born

I heard afterwards
That no one came
To get me
Meanwhile the birthday was a success
The children played
Internment camp
And to finish
Stood the youngest up and shot him

Windows

For four months
I haven't dared enter
My own home

Riding by
On the bus
I see lights in the window

Times like these
The absurd is so close

Chasm

The first day of spring
And life goes on almost normal
The second channel back on radio
And with Frank Sinatra crooning
Life goes on almost normal
There are fewer patrols
Even curfew has its merits
And despite the layers of dialectic
I am still almost always free
Prisoners swarm in their jail cells
Like termites in a chunk of wood
And surely you've heard that in the provinces
Officers are drinking themselves to an early grave
While at a police station in Katowice
They beat somebody up and in Poznan
This guy just got through dying
Meanwhile next to a wall in Wujek coal mine
A cross just sprouted its first buds
But nothing strange in that since it's March
A month almost free
And between the words
Almost and *free*
Is this chasm
If you want to jump over
Try flying out head first

Alarm

Pass it on
Almost two hundred years
This printing press has fallen
This group has been arrested
The tempest brews over C.
And K. is judged a traitor
On guard on guard
Pass it on
Once again Poland is being tested
An informer listens
At the same set of doors
On the walls they slap red paint
Over the scribbled words of freedom
Into the twenty-first century children
Smuggle pamphlets in their schoolbags
On guard on guard
Pass it on
To the borders and beyond
Alarm alarm

Our Grammar

Subject--the one that got fingered
Negative--the one no longer with us
Direct Object--straight in the face
Indirect Object--any number of tools
Instrumental for torture
Locative--here on the Vistula
Its broken back
A muffled scream
Our hands almost paralyzed
This grammar
Is too hard to learn in one life
Surrounded by horrible case endings
Inflexible parts of speech
Words
Their pins pulled out and ticking

Used Straw

From the building next door
They hauled out a worker
History will not forgive you—he said
But except for a child playing on the stairwell
The words fell on deaf ears
The men slapped him in handcuffs
Four of them one of him
Thousands of people brewed tea down the block
And the December snow fell

And we who are schooled
In the relativity between hard objects and ideas
Realize history
Comes in more than one version
Like the one composed by the neighborhood spy
Where our minds are used straw they spread in the fields
Over which they sprinkle broken up brick
Or lay asphalt and concrete

And someday a child
If possible
Will build a great house
Of cards from a marked deck

Beasts

They say our Madonna in Zyrardow
Has joined the party
They open her I.D.
To show the photo
And the two scars on her cheek

They say Christ in Bialoleka Prison
Signed an oath of loyalty
On TV they turn the camera
On a pale white sheet
With a red smudge

They say the twelve apostles petitioned
To dissolve Solidarity
Holed up in their office
They break out the mineral water
And only one is sad

Now there is ironclad proof
Even the cross won't deny the rights of state
Or that the Star of Bethlehem was red

While we the steadfast
Tough and disbelieving
Are thrown to the beasts
Of lies   betrayal   hyprocrisy

The Detention Camp

(a poem for a book published under censorship)

Among these lines of poetry
Are patches of white
Surrounded by barbed wire

Inside the whiteness strangers and friends
Walk around in a circle

Titles commandeered into watchtowers
Where the sentries keep one eye on the prisoners
And one finger tapping on their guns

20

*City**

The streets of my city are my streets
There where a dog lifts a leg and latches
Himself to a tree with a golden stream
And the wind kicks up the scent of brown hair
From a girl I no longer remember

There you can still see ruts from the tanks
On the October asphalt of 1956
The passage of people who came to add
Their blood to the Hungarian revolt

And always at the end a blind corridor
I run down on a December night
Instead of a war torch a black icicle in my hands

The streets of my city are no longer mine
Dusklight cut into triangles
Falling on a small prison stool
And in our apartments stacked up like bunkbeds
We sleep every night
The barbed wire running through our fingers

Daybreak the city unfolds
Wadded and grimy
Like a warrant for my arrest
And am I really the one who scurries
From trench to trench
With a newborn poem in my teeth
Am I really the man alone at his desk
With his head doubled in a fist

*1956, the year of the Hungarian Revolution, also saw unrest in Poland,
including the massacre by government troops of five striking workers in Poznan.

Zomo*

These unhappy beasts were grabbed
From boarded up windows
From the broken necks of bottles
They were issued teargas guns and bats
And let off the leash

They lope for the meat on our backs
The soft spots on our skulls
While swaying in their matted fur
The Mother of God
Keeps rocking her dead baby

*Zomo (an acronym stemming from "Zmobolizowane Oddzialy Milicji Obywatelskiej," or "Mobilized Units of the Citizen's Militia") was the popular name for the members of the special riot units used for the first time by the Polish authorities at the beginning of martial law and thereafter to squelch unrest. In breaking up strikes, street demonstrations and other forms of protest, the Zomo quickly earned a reputation for brutality, handling the dirty work the government feared the regular police corps and army would refuse to carry out. The Zomo were composed of individuals from questionable backgrounds, including former criminals and suspended policemen.

Alms

I forgot about Romek
He got five years
I forgot about so many
That now I don't even remember
Who it was I forgot
What can be done what can I do
So they won't be deserted
On their iron-bar archipelagos
Only from time to time
They stand before me
Line after line as if for roll call
As I try to slip past
I'm in a hurry
I have an appointment to keep
Their gaze pasted on the back of my neck
Warm and sticky
Like a split comb of honey
What can be done what can I do
An appointment I have to keep
So I throw them this hurried poem
My alms
For a hand clenched in a fist

Monuments*

A monument was built from flowers
So how can they spoil
What is already torn and withered

A plaque was dedicated on a square
The plaque is gone
But the hole that remains
Is a monument

So what will our keepers do next
When even a hole in the earth
Becomes a monument
When the air becomes a monument
What will they do next
When they themselves are monuments to shadow
What will they do next

*Despite occasional destruction by the authorities, throughout martial law in Poland a flower cross was maintained in the courtyard of St. Anne's Church near the Old Town in Warsaw by various people (mainly elderly women) sympathetic to Solidarity. Victory Square had been the previous site for the cross--until the square was closed for "repairs" shortly before the imposition of martial law in December 1981.

Elevator

Three guys came after Dad an hour ago
Three guys came but don't get too nervous
I've cleared out the apartment
The bookshelves are clean
But Mom still hasn't made it back
She's probably okay though
I hear they've quit taking mothers
But maybe you should leave
They could always come back
But don't get too nervous

I ended up plenty nervous
The elevator I rode didn't stop
On the ground but kept going
Floor after floor into the earth

Freedom

They stopped me
Read over my name my number
The tattooed ink of my I.D.
Then let me go
As if I were completely innocent
They must have been blind
Not to notice my eyes
Were blazing with light
Two greenhorn policemen

I walked away free
Dragging streets like a giant chain behind me

Polish Dogs

The dogs get thrown on the street
Because there is no meat
Because our own stringy hearts
Are rationed
Because nothing makes any sense
When everyone's home gets ground to rubble
There is no corner left for feeling
The dogs get thrown on the street
Let them raise hind-legs to the curfew
Their howls and their bristling fur
Crazed loyalty in their deep brown eyes
Let them cart from the trash heaps
Our unfinished bones
And scatter our decaying flesh any place they can

And should these dogs die
Out of hunger and despair
Far from the exalted doorstep of national tragedy
Let's keep a porchlight shining
In our eyes
The round eyes of the sinking Titanic

Pulp

No cost was too great
To save the core of the nation

So they hid
The core under the bed
Tried to avoid patrols and sensitive topics

Decades passed before they checked

Just a sea of pulp
In which two eyeballs swam
And a wedding ring
Stuck on somebody's finger

Possessed*

In the Polish National Theater
Extravaganza
For Polish-Soviet friendship
A poetry recital
Someone played a polka on a squeezebox
The ladies' choir sang
Then the limousines streamed off
The guards disappeared
Leaving an empty theater
A stage on which Konrad
Rushed up and down
Wringing his hands in a frenzy
Gray-haired   shrivelled   possessed

*Konrad was the tragic hero of Polish Romantic poet Adam Mickiewicz's epic drama, *Forefathers Eve*. This distinctly anti-Russian play, since its first publication in 1823, has faced censorship from both Czarist and Soviet Moscow. It was banned from performance as late as 1968, when the closure of a Warsaw University production sparked severe disturbances amongst college students nationwide.

Echoes

Clouds lured out onto the lake
The red roof on a hut
Blazes back at the sky

All quiet in the village
While in the cities
The parades are routed down
Into the nation's dark craters

All quiet in the village
Only over the water there carries
The sound of pounding nails so clearly
You feel it in your hand

Milk

In this crazy country
Where an uprising has never yet
Made it off the ground
Where the dead carry more weight than the living
Where truth and ideas turn skin and bone
Only the moths swell up like cows
And provide for our children
Black bitter milk

In this country we wither
Needing watered we get blood

A Call for Peace

And after everyone
Has been found guilty
On the slight technicality
Judge jury evidence are false
True peace will reign in the land
Old women will not grumble
As they keel over in line
Strikes will not stop production
Of defective body parts
The weary nation will close its eyes
And bask on the cemetery lawn

Each Night

Curfew
Counts my ribs and vertebrae
Its face pasted to my window
Its eyes locked in mine

Warsaw sliced in half
By the looks of informers
The factories like busted teeth
The gates to the university
Ripped out like a tongue

Our silence
Floats over the city
Smoke and dust
After everything is leveled

Five Year Plan

> And we lowly eaters of bread
> They'll make over into angels.
> —"Testament," Julian Slowacki (1809-1849)

Today they try to change
Our desire for bread
Into an appetite for lies
Anyone who chokes
Will be baked in the loaf as well

Single File*

Parades black from mourning
And the grime of time
Keep marching
From 1861 till today

Once again
They hang Traugutt
From a 200 zloty bill

Once again the only way out
From a dead end
Is up the alley
To another brick wall

And the last parade
Is when we line up single file
To be issued gall and a sprig of thorns
Each one his own white sheet

*In February 1861, one hundred people were killed in Warsaw during a march and demonstration for greater Polish independence from Czarist Russia. This event in part prepared the way for the full-scale January Uprising of 1863. For several months Romuald Traugutt headed the shadow government of Poland, which despite repeated setbacks in the field, still managed to function until Traugutt's apprehension and execution by hanging. A pre-Soviet and thus "safe" Polish hero, Traugutt is now on the 200-zloty banknote of the People's Republic of Poland.

The Front

From now on
We must be more stringent
In our educational aims

We give the children an extra
Sandwich for the road
A nervous tug on their backpacks

We watch them walk
Without us
Off to the front lines

Defeat

In the end we have to live
With the fact we lost

The house is still intact
The flowers still grow
On the cement balcony
We use the same words as always

But yet the floor shifts beneath us
The blooms are strange and
Our words run a high fever
With blood welling in their eyes

The White Meadow Prison Diary

Prison

Beat on us lie to us make us bored
Make us bored lie to us beat on us
It seems there's no way out
You can't jump through the bars
And they've taken away our shoestrings and belts
They only left the walls
And beyond the walls
Socialism
As far as the eye can see
For a long time looking out
You could see the treetops
But now everything is
Plastered flat

*Interrogation with Map**

Your father is dying
One official tells me
And I can hear how an i-v feeds
The steady drip into one's last poem
You're the one killing him he adds
Because you went into hiding
Because you had your hand in the underground
I keep watching his skull
The skin stretched over an object
And the map of Poland hanging opposite
A gilded bust of Feliks Dzierzynski
In the spot where once pulsed Warsaw

*Mieczyslaw Jastrun, a poet and critic recognized as one of the most important writers in 20th century Polish literature, died a few weeks after his son Tomasz returned from martial law detention. Feliks Dzierzynski was the head of *Cheka*, the ruthless secret police operating during the early years of Soviet Russia. Polish-born, he is considered by most Poles to be a traitor to both country and humanity.

Rings

It's November 1982
118 people
Live in Cell Block 3
Steel-worker
Architect
Pipe-fitter from Ursus Tractors
Pediatrician
Diamond cutter
And I the poet
That's all there is to it
118 blue-collar
Workers on mind and matter
And a hallway
For a common backbone
Vertebrae working loose
Like rings going outward in big blue water

Board*

Andrzej Gwiazda gave me a board
Who would have thought
The pleasure
An ordinary board could furnish

I made a shelf
Above my bed
On the shelf went my books
All one of them

Rebuilding the world
From scratch

*Andrzej Gwiazda was a member of the Solidarity Central Committee. He remained in detention through most of martial law.

Shipwreck

The snowy beach of December
Here in Bialoleka
From the wreck of one more revolution
Wash up 118 people
Ribs sticking out from lack of freedom
Poland frozen on their tongues

Planet*

This one is here for the reason
He switched on the machine room siren
Screaming like it was skinned alive
This one is here for the reason
He couldn't keep a job
But kept mumbling the word freedom
This one is here for the reason
He deserted the wheel of his bus
On the busy intersection
Between the Old and New World
This one is here for the reason
He clammed up when they started to beat him

These guys pack the jails
Where did so much life originate
On such a dead planet

*Nowy Swiat, New World Avenue, is a major Warsaw street.

Tread

So at last
Power is in the hands of the proletariat
Our present goal is a jail ruled by justice
We split up the bread and margerine
Each according to his needs
And during our daily walks
We take a spin on the bare tread of history

Hat

This older gentleman
Also takes walks in the Yard
But his hat clashes
With the barbed wire
With the bars muzzling the windows
As if they were afraid we might bite through
This man with the hat
Is here because he was seeking
To overthrow the government by force
And violate our treaties

Sixty years old
His hands furrowed like the earth
Of pre-war Europe
And a very dangerous hat
On his head

Small Fires

Amidst our silence our children
Run without sound
Our wives rise up
To wipe the haze from the afternoon
We lie with our mouths open
Our thoughts aglow
Like the light through a kitchen door

Prose

When they lock me up
I used to say
I'm going to write poems
Well they locked me up
But the words
Just won't lie down in a line
Everyone here just talks prose
A few simple hard-headed words
Repeated over and over again

Visiting Day

My son today was for the first time
In a prison
Already he knows what the gate looks like
The watchtowers
And he knows how much I miss him
That leave-taking
Is like a ripped up piece of paper
On which he had drawn
A sun and a house

The Present Day

In Cell #12
The Medievalist Karol Modzelewski
Has a lecture
On the origins of the Polish state
An audience of tractor mechanics
Tool-cutters
And a meteorologist
Who referees sports on the side
Poland's beginnings
Are shrouded in darkness
Tomorrow is nothing more
Than wind whistling through a chopped virgin forest
And the present day like a rabbit
Scampers through a barren field

Fatherland

He has been here a year
His wife a bag of tears
His father dies slowly
His own soldiers
Have shot his brother
Beat his son unconscious
And should a truth flare up
They take care of it
With a shot of phenolbarbital

And the fatherland
Has anyone word
From the fatherland

Rhymes

Who has time for poetry here
And yet something rhymes
Between what we say
And what a century before
Wrote Norwid Slowacki Mickiewicz

Silence

They have already said everything
Polish poets of the nineteenth century
The only thing remaining is the silence
We fill with the contents of our stomachs

Chain

His forefathers sat in jail
For Poland
Which wasn't there

His father sat in jail
For Poland
Which rose up

Now he sits in jail
For Poland
Which didn't make it

The Evening News*

*I don't know what I'd do
If it wasn't for the special squads*
This old lady testifies on TV
We laugh ourselves to tears
Even though we know
The salt will remain long after
The laughter burns off

*During the period of martial law in Poland, the special riot squads (Zomo) were often portrayed in the government media as performing functions other than riot-control and strike-breaking, including caring for the sick and aged.

Schools

I always knew I was destined for no good
Says this assembly line worker from Ursus Tractors
That's why I never felt fear
And I never had trouble
Sleeping

Now cast on the shore he watches
The schools of dead fish float past
Underneath the wreckage of a bridge
And the factories
Sitting there in silence

Removing a Farmer*

Today they hauled Heniek Trebacz
Away to jail

Back home they wait in vain
Cows full of the fields
The organ he played
In the country church

His bed is mussed up
By someone else
Someone else goes out
For a short stroll

And although five plainclothed angels
And three in sacred-blue uniform
Watch over him
No one helps him drag his cross

*The word in Polish for this type of farmer, as in Russian, is "kulak," and designates a class of prosperous farmer/peasants. In the Soviet Union, especially under Stalin, such individuals' properties were targeted for collectivization--and the owners murdered. During martial law, rural activists were interned and otherwise persecuted as well.

Him

No wings
Only a sunken breast
The post office censor
Looks through our letters
When he bends over the deep chasms of words
His medals start swaying
Like the Martyrs of the Revolution
About whom we can no longer. . .

Light

Already we've worn down the guards
They're puzzled by our words
And our silence
That's why every night at ten
They shut off the lights
For a few hours the situation
Will be clear

Mouse

In someone's heart the twist of a key
The turn of a lock opens
Or closes for years
A century
Paces the corridor
And a gray mouse gnaws
At the wall of tragedy

Rat

We're not free
Those who guard us aren't free
Like this frustrated interrogator
The bars and windows aren't free
The sheet metal beaten
Down to the marrow of each door
The only thing free
Is the rat
Who this night left name and address
In the cupboard on the yellow cheese

Free

Some are now being turned free
Which has an irony of its own
We say goodbye our palms
Open and close like the door
We watch them walk out
Their shoulders
Stooped with the weight
Of a dead brother or sister

Christmas Eve

Already common knowledge
Not everyone will go home

Today we take a hike
Through nature
Says the warder we call Liver

A clump of weeds is what he means
And we watch as in the sky above us
Christmas Eve blows away

Reunion

Practically everyone's saying
They will keep up the struggle
But a few intend
To grow strawberries

A berry flushes redder
With the blood of the fallen
And turning to dew on the leaves
Are the tears of those who remember

So someday we shall all meet again
In a patch under one roof of the mouth

The Fall

Only 27 prisoners remain
We melt away like a giant icicle
That could have cracked their heads
But now drips slowly on their helmets

In the Exercise Yard

Everyone clustered
Around a muddy ditch
Looking at the gray veins of clay
The wet sand collapsing
Everyone was mystified
They felt the pull
Of earth

Ehh--Someone spoke
That there is Poland
And without a word
Each went his own way

Last Supper

Thirteen of us still not released
A full table
Though missing
Are Christ and Judas
Victims of a cruel death

And we the living
Are joined together
To share our lost cause
The hand
With the rusted nail

52

Before Transport

December 18, 1982
In cell #19 they hold
The last meeting of Solidarity
Imported chocolate
The perfect globe of an orange
Its skin ripped open with teeth
From the next world war

Transport*

They hauled off five to permanent arrest
Seweryn stopped reading a poem
Janek yelled through the bars
They won't break me
You guys keep fanning the flames
Grzegorz asked us to send his wishes
To friends on the outside
Not a peep out of Andrzej and Karol

And as they were driven
Over the damp
Cold skin of the city
A silhouette in a window
Cut bread with an artificial arm
Someone on the street carried a Christmas tree
Bleeding a pool of shadow

And we who stay
Eight hopeless men
Wait listening in the hole
We've tunneled under Europe

*Jastrun was released under a general amnesty on December 22, 1982. Only five Bialoleka internees, all members of the Solidarity Central Committee, were formally charged with crimes against the state and transported to a regular prison.

Leaving Prison

There was no one to greet me
Only a unit of angels fingering their nightsticks
It was dark some people in a hurry
The end of a bus line wrapped around my neck
The drivers in between their rounds were drinking vodka
Complaining—Nothing is ours anymore
I thought maybe the world had changed
But it was easy to be mistaken
I walked down the street avoiding
The cracks between the wobbly slabs of sidewalk
On the corner a grocer at a stand
Was circumsizing carrots
My own neighbor didn't recognize me
He didn't know how I looked in a gray beard
As I reached my door I heard a rustle
My wife and son were rolling out the red carpet
A tangled ball of wool
On the floor slick as ice

Return

I felt each hug on my neck
Like a large and small wreath
Plaited by my wife and son
The furniture didn't know me
Nor did the walls
Only the window chopped through
To hard reality
Approached and looked right through my eyes
Into the darkness beyond

54

A Time for Remembrance and Forgetting

Underneath the Leaf

What am I doing here
In Morocco
Not alone but with no one either
Allah is great
Wrote the Berbers on the mountainside
And I
Who am I
In this hotel
On the fourth floor
In this leaky room
An insect afraid of rain
Who goes underneath the leaf
Of this poem

Gotland

I saw the Viking's bare skull
On the half-shell of his helmet
His eyes perfect and empty
His straight yellow hair
Perfect and empty
His mother's name inside his mouth
Changed into a small stone
His teeth disturbingly complete
The strong teeth of a young boy
The same age as my son
This man buried here in the cradle
Of a mass grave
I saw it all as if
In the palm of my hand
My very own hand
As the landscape began to roll up
into one tangled ball of wool

Babel

Lamb of God who takes away the world's sins
Have mercy on us

Shepherd who comes with a knife
Have mercy on us

The lamb has vanished
No trace of the shepherd

The knife passes from hand to hand
A brick

For the last floor of the Tower

In every window
A question without answer
In every question
A human face

Leaving the House

I wake up too early
And I don't feel like talking
The birds
Feathered hearts from another world
Already converse with the trees and sky

I dress as if I am pulling
A stranger's body to me
The kettle sings of the miraculous change
Of water into air

On the radio twenty degrees
Below zero
In the Persian Gulf another tanker
Sinks with its cargo of hope

I walk out onto the street
Follow the path I myself have hollowed
From the asphalt and stone
To the place where I meet you
Its steamy fragrance
Of coffee and tea
O my delicate ladybug
Cling to me tighter
The female musk of my death

Guardian Angel

I felt his hot breath
On my neck
As I ran up the narrow staircase
Flight after flight

But then he tripped
And fell

As far as Icarus
With a dagger of sunlight
In his back

Today all that remains
Is his body dried in a schoolbook
A giant butterfly
With the twisted face of an injured child

Today the ones who follow me around
Have walkie-talkies instead of hearts
The small change of their humanity
Rattling in their pockets
From what kind of heaven did they fall

Forty Eight Hours*

(May 1984)

I ran you in because you wrote
A poem about me
Says with a smile this captain
Of the secret police

In cell number five
Two warmhearted criminals
Tell me their lives
One stole a bicycle
The other strangled his uncle in Praga

In the corridor two warmhearted policemen
Give a man a beating
I listen to the argument of club and skin
How they eventually come to an understanding

On the floor above us a typewriter
Taps out the specialty of the house
Cigarette butts join a scrap of newspaper
To proclaim our friendship with the Empire

The rustle of women's legs
From the basement window on Malczewski
A street named for a Romantic poet and mountain-climber

Then I chip a hole
To the next cell
Some communists from the nineteenth-century
Are still serving time
There is so much to tell
But I keep silent
They wouldn't believe me anyway
Their eyes fixed on the future
As their fingers slide the rosary
The hollow seed of the dialectic

I'm turned loose at six
Warsaw awakens
I kneel down to re-lace its shoes
I get up with a shiver
A sigh of relief so shallow
That today or tomorrow
Fording the river with ease
Will be a Cossack patrol

    *The captain in stanza one is referring to Jastrun's poem "Interrogation with Map," written in Bialoleka Prison. In the 1980s, each year "unofficial" May Day parades and populist celebrations of the 18th-century Third of May Constitution (a democratic constitution adopted by Poland right before its invasion and partition by Russia, Austria and Prussia) formed a challenge to the government's monopoly on historical interpretation. Frequently during this period in early May, opposition figures were rounded up by the police and held, legally, up to forty-eight hours without any official charges having to be made.

*The Captive Dream**

And once again before dawn a police search
This time the Czar's gendarmes
I thought the place was clean
But they sling my complete set of Mickiewicz on the floor
I yell it's published after World War II
But the two-headed eagles on their shoulders shrug
"Time like Siberia has no borders"
Only the ring of the telephone scatters them
And they start circling
In the the flock of crows above our building

On the line is a friend
Did you hear
They're running people in
Get the hell out of your apartment right away

But where am I to go
On Szucha Street the SS pull fingernails
A block away is the KGB
The 80s slope down like flatlands
Into the depths of God knows what
But this is familiar terrain I've been here before
Where I hide my books in panic
And hide myself the First and Third of May
Yet I always return
Where I tiptoe from room to room
Afraid to turn on the lights
A lit match in my hand until
I find Poland curled in my bed asleep
With the shoelaces removed from its shoes
The crows still circle above the building
And as if to toy with me the crowbar rifle fist
Pauses before knocking on the door

*Adam Mickiewicz, one of Poland's foremost Romantic poets and a crusader for national independence during the time of the Polish partitions, after World War II for the most part came to be considered safe reading by the Communist Polish authorities. But, during the Czarist years, his works were certainly contraband. The Russian imperial insignia was that of a two-headed eagle. During World War II, Szucha Boulevard was the site of the central Gestapo post in Warsaw .

A Letter from Prison

Locked inside Poland
I pace the streets
I've learned not to stumble
On the dead
To not get my feet wet
Trudging through uprising after uprising

Locked on the fourth floor
I wear a path from the door to the window
Past the hungry potted plants
The gray spines of my books

Locked inside your arms
I touch your thigh
And wait for the waves to rise up
And erase the edges of my body

Locked in my poems I stutter
Through too many things at once

My young son runs into the room
I hug him to me
But how
Can I keep away the flames
By using warmth myself

The Last Days of My Guardian Angel

Out of the blue my guardian angel dropped by
He wasn't daunted by my age
Or my sceptical smile

As he sat across from me in silence
I noticed that his wings were gone
He was breathing too quickly
And stunk of vodka and cigarettes
He was old and living on borrowed time

He sat across from me in silence
But I didn't need words to understand
That the heavens outside my window were empty
That the only sound left was the murmur of stars
The dying bees of the universe
Still going about their work

Ground Cover

The lesser evil flourishes
And already stretches
From the hilltops down
To the free will lying low
Is anyone left with the nerve
To say the wrong crop was planted

The Great Emigration

And in the end they emigrate
Into their lungs their livers their stomachs
They cultivate the taste buds on their tongues
And excite the animals in their bodies

But at some point they return
Changed beyond recognition
Here where the trees grow old
But not necessarily wise

In Mourning (1983)*

Your funeral travelled in another procession
Our mourning was part of more mourning
Your absence like the funnel
For steel to flow
Into the black die of our hope
Here in the landscape of shortage
The kitchen light burns
With dark murky colors
And the birds that eat
The seeds we scatter
Watch us with the unfriendly eyes
Of the imprisoned and the forgotten

*As mentioned previously, Tomasz Jastrun's father, Mieczyslaw Jastrun, died in early 1983, soon after the son's release from the Bialoleka detention camp.

Vacation

Uncertain shape of bed and chair
Painful depression in the upholstery
Rubbed by the back of his head

Dead weight of hanging suits
Crevices of pockets and sleeves
Tunnels no longer travelled
By the trains of arms and legs

Only words winging like swallows
From between the pages of a book
The terrible whir from the mother tongue

Otherwise shells crumbs husks
How from these scraps can we rig
An excuse for ourselves
To sail off on the vacation of life

*Eyes**

In Powazki National Cemetery
Black cats run wild
One crouches on the grave of Lesmian
Another stares my father in the eyes

Clinging to each other
Are flowers with sliced veins

And like the hearts of gray mice
The inscriptions on stone and marble
Beat faster
The names and dates of birth and death

I leave there with my hands empty
With my skull almost bare
A thought flickers through the eyeballs like a torch
Dies and flares again
There is no city around this graveyard
But a graveyard circles around the town
And the eyes of the cats loom
Over the last one hundred years

*Powazki National Cemetery is the burial place of many major Polish artistic and political figures, including poets Boleslaw Lesmian, Leopold Staff, and Tomasz Jastrun's father, Mieczyslaw Jastrun.

Fruitless

He left socks and shirts
A sweater still warm
As he moved to the most beautiful
Part in all of Warsaw

He lives next door to Leopold Staff
Within eyesight is Boleslaw Lesmian
Whom he hasn't seen in ages

Chestnuts fall from the trees at my feet
As if they want something from me
But lack the power to ask
And I am just as fruitless wearing his warm sweater
I might as well be bringing him water
Trying to cup my leaking hands
Because I am so close
Though I cannot reach him
Through these tricky graveyard paths
The doors no one can open

So I go home to his poems
In each the light is on
We sit together in the kitchen
The windows open-wide
Water boils on the stove for tea
The limb of an acacia taps
Wants something
But lacks the power to ask

Lights

I never fathomed his death
A muddied long-poem
I couldn't finish
Something never written
I was unable to grasp
A book still smouldering from a fire

But at night I can glimpse
In the darkness between the pages of his books
The trains of stanzas swaying on their journey
The glow of light from the compartments
The ideas cramped and weary
The throb of wheels and unending
Babble of conversation and the sudden
Lurch forward of a memory
Stopped by a jerk of the hand
As if a lock of gray hair had fallen
Down in my father's eyes

Nothing

If I forget for a moment my father's death
I start to walk down blindly
The streets of an unknown city

And suddenly I am faced
With the house where my father grew up
The fragrant stairs inside
And the smooth wooden handrails

And when I take his book from the shelf
A bird flies from the pages
To perch on the edge of my endurance

Not far off a new housing district
Gets built by frozen hands
Slab by concrete slab

And I feel the hair rise on my neck
Because always in the presence of death
The most frightening thing
Is that practically nothing has taken place

Stony Brook on Long Island*

This elderly pair says my eyes
Are the spitting image of my father's

My father's eyes are closed

This thought
Flutters so quietly
Between us unsaid
That for the first time
I see bone start to show
Silence
Bleached white
By the current of time

They hand me a photo

A young man
He has to be my father
I recognize
The young woman as well

Their legs bare
Knees like little mirrors
In a dark room

The blunt edge
Of my father's smile
Cuts to the bone

The photographer
A writer still living
His life spent aloft
Between Warsaw and Paris

We discuss who has died from cancer
How he himself is much weaker
An electronic bug stimulates his heart
When we say goodbye his hand
Rustles in mine
Like the page of a poem
Crumpled and tossed down in despair

74

And as if this was not enough
Today I turned thirty-five
Easy as going downhill
To the river where as a child I caught fish
Their round eyes full of sadness and surprise

(September 1985, New York)

Our Children of the Emigration

Our children learn more quickly
The spry young animal in their mouths
Climbs high in the branches
While the autumn leaves of the mother tongue
Lie swamped under asphalt
Heading off for the Brooklyn Bridge
The cars like a flooded river to Manhattan
Long arms of skyscrapers raised in the sky
As if to pluck them down a star

Our children stray the farthest
At some point vanishing into the landscape
Like a small stone picked up and tossed
And only occasionally someone will stumble over
An unpronouncable first name
Until the tongue wears down its rough edges

Our children indeed come out best
Abandoning our worries
They become like a flock of birds
Flying off
To gather brightly colored plastic for their nest

That's why I'm so sad
As I watch these children play
In this giant backyard called America
This other planet
Happier than mine

But feelings like these I must squeeze like fruit
Till only there remains the bitter pit
Only blood and bone

(New York, August 1985)

76

The Cry

So few things matter
You can put them up against each other
Or string them from a cross
Hunger sex laughter
Love and pain
A road leading to a house
A bed and table
We two and him
Born just yesterday
His cry in the next room
Like the tail of a comet
Brushing the stars

Father and Son

Here is not good enough
And he looks at me with reproach
But what can I do
I'm not about to offer excuses
So I let my silence speak
Finally he hugs me
As if he suddenly realizes
We have to get along
To come to an agreement
There is no one else
To deal with

And after a while
We both get to work
He collects
Old bus tickets
I fuss with words
Out of which I can whittle
My crutches and cane

Live Shells

Their son inhabited
A different planet
And they were naive
When he asked about the dead
They responded that no one dies
They only go to sleep
But he was more clever than that
He killed spiders and ants
And examined the agonies of the butterfly

When he stopped his questions
They sighed with relief
But he pried answers for himself
From the firing squad wall

He fingered the shells for years
Until he put them in his pocket
Draped a gun on his shoulder
And headed off to war

Children and Soldiers

The soldier tenses
As he guards the hothouse
Where blood red flowers
Bloom for the pleasure of colonels

Children press their cheeks
To the cold wire of the fence
And yell that a ladybug
Crawls the green meadow
Of the soldier's fatigues
It comes to a halt
Directly over the heart
Snapped shut by a cheap metal button

The soldier keeps mum
Rocking the greedy baby
He has strapped to his back
The long dark throat
And automatic tongue

Tending One's Garden

This retired barber
Is ruthless
As he tends his garden
The soil enriched by the last war
He cuts the veins on the roses
Slaughters aphids
When exhausted he props himself up
On his instruments of torture
To peer through the chain link fence
And eavesdrop
Could the time be ripe
To bring the rest of the world
Under the reach of his hoe

In a great ring around him
Behind the bars of their own fences
Stand his neighbors
The young the old
Equally greedy and watchful
Pulling out words as well as weeds

Peasant Farmer

He sits in the wooden doorway
Sighs—one more day

Eighty years old
The blows of his axe
Made this door from a tree
The morning from the summer
And from the morning he squeezes out a sigh

He peers down the throat of the world
Through the broken teeth of the fence

He gets up
Plows his fields by the forest
Or by the house
The furrows in his brow

And when he finishes with the feeding
Of every pig in the world
The milking of every cow
He buries his wife
Old and gnarled as he

He sticks out
Like a thumb
He banged with a hammer

He sits down in the wooden doorway
Sighs—one more night

Preparing for Bed

Slide a piece of furniture
And no shadow remains
The space that each object takes up
Is indifferent

But the place that you inhabited
Still whispers
The mirror
Where you once combed your hair
Flushes red and white like your skin

Tonight while preparing for bed
I forgot once again
To wind my memory

And now I can't recall the shade
Of your dress
Always riding up

Eyebrows

With dry lips
I brushed her mouth
But nothing happened
She didn't slap me
Her eyes didn't change color
Only the brows
Stirred
Like the wings of a bird
Deciding
To fold against the body
Or keep going

Fog

Time and space herd
Us toward our first meeting
A door
And a short hallway that leads
To your hand
Held out to mine
Beyond is a room
I have yet to know
A table
I have never sat at
I become lost
In fog
The color of your eyes
And knock over a shelf
Full of things fragile and irreplacable

Paying a Visit

Warm sea of hair
Pouring through the teeth of the comb
Soft skin of a towel
Soap slick from sliding on my body
And a mirror which suddenly has no memory
I am the only one left
With a twisted face that is not mine

I change it before I walk into the kitchen

It is not your arms but your eyes
That hold me across the table
They rest on my unease
As if waiting at a station

And a train pulls in without a screech
To a wordless platform
On each coach the windows glow
But go out in the blackness of the swaying tea
You place recklessly on the table

Our Table of Desire

We sit across from each other
A knife and warm bread
Water boils in the teapot
Hunger sprouts in our eyes

Don't look at me that way
We'll clean up the dishes
You'll scrape the crumbs
Into your open palm
The door I close when leaving
Will keep silent when he returns

In the Kitchen

She scrubs each utensil
As if preparing for surgery
She goes to the freezer
To pull out her heart
And chuckles at us coldly

I watch my son
His crayon version of the world
In the beginning there is the sun
Stick men born in torment
Twisted legs and faces

For years now
Snow
Has been falling in me
Covering every window and door
But if I tried to leave I know
I would be frozen
On the threshold

Coming To

Their muzzles beat on the wooden stakes
The city burns in their eyes
Throw them their firstborn
To devour
Gag yourself with your pen
Vomit out Rome
The damned Tiber
Has changed its course

Their paws have gone to sleep
And the muzzles resting on the paws
Eyes stuck shut
With ash and sand
Rome lies in a pool
Drying on the tiled floor

Wake up
The river turns into the Vistula
The woman you loved comes into view
Captured in an arrangement of violets

The Rose

Time caked between my fingers
Out my window the concrete slabs of Stegny and Ursynow
Rise like tombstones for our children
A car sputters to a stop
The wind scratches at the underfed trees
And here I am at my desk with a poem
That doesn't want to live
A blind fool with busted out teeth
Time caked between my fingers

And above me opens
Each frightening petal
The wild rose
Of the universe

Seed

Birds
Fly in the raised window of our lives
Their wings
Open and close
In panic

Birds
fly in the dim-lit hallway

They land on our shoulders
Dead from exhaustion
Hungry

Our hands empty
They search our eyes and mouth
For seed

Uncertain Ground

My poems are ready
To explode with distrust
Even I tread lightly
And stay on the marked paths

This minefield was laid
Before I was born
On the edge of some prehistoric ocean
In a war of words against other words
Struggling in vain to touch God

Small Grains

I don't like long poems

A short poem is like a stone
You can clench in your hand
Aim like a ball
Swallow before bedtime

Long poems are like streets
Where cars line the sidewalks
And people languish before store windows

A short poem fits in a breath
An open or closed fist
A short gasp and moan

Long poems are
Lost in the whitewash
Noise upon noise

A short poem bides its time
The small grain of what we know

Early in the Day

Today my neighbor
Is once again at the piano
But his Chopin
Does not lift me up

Instead the staircase of sound
Leads me to the basement
Where the dead are hidden
Under clumps of sidewalk and asphalt

I shield my eyes and return to my room

Out the window they plant a cross
Over our latest defeat
On its outstretched arms of steel
Already women have hung
Our bedsheets and diapers to dry

*Our Lady of Helplessness**

Our lady of helplessness
Beats out the path
I walk daily
For coal and water

I turn the lights on and off
I wash my face and hands in ashes
Gaze deep into the furnace
Like it was my soul

Our lady of helplessness
Has premature gray hair
At times on the stairs
She runs out of breath

It gets harder and harder to write
A poem she likes
Great tragedies or lyrics
Of the decomposing present

But if I stop for a second
I hear the chorus of eunuchs
"Poland Has Not Yet Perished"
And so I keep writing to drown them out
When they sing "We Are Still Living"

*The Polish National Anthem, written during the years of the partition, starts out: "Poland has not yet perished/As long as we are still living."

Scrap

After us will be neither scrap metal
Nor a laugh
From beginning to end
We have had no illusions
All our uprisings
Lie packed in the foyer
Along with a toothbrush
And towel

When someone knocks on the door
The echo
Pounds through the empty years
But there is no call to action
No convoy to Siberia
Only the upstairs neighbor whose sink
Once again has overflowed
He comes wringing his hands to warn us

Our Black Madonna of Czestochowa

Varicose veins big as the Vistula
She waits in line

Her sad eyes of the Orient
The two scars on her right cheek

And though she holds a child in one arm
No one lets her go ahead

In a Cage

Our eagle no longer
Roams wild in the mountains
Everyone can keep one
In their own home

Cage gilded or silver-plated
Feathers painted red
Claws and beak clipped off
Like a parrot it repeats
The same words again

And only the wrinkles
Around its weary eyes betray
Its thousand years of flight
Over this devastated land

A School in No One's Name

Someone opens the window
During the Polish history lesson

The smell of scorched eggs
Wafts into the room
A page from a burning book flutters
Like the wings on a dove

The circuit of stars on the blackboard

No one knows the answer

Behind their desks old women
And even older men
Drop like flies

The window slams shut
The lesson goes on

The Year 1864

Forest empty as the echo
Of the last volley
On the moss a red bandage

The members of the uprising are in heaven
Or on the road to Siberia

The days in broken ranks
Line up
For the long march into history

It takes place far away
But still in Europe
In an open book
Which fell from the shelf

On the next page
The Vistula gapes like a wound

Road

The tree lined highway
Traveled by a carriage
A man with pince-nez
And black top hat
Passes a house
Lamp in the open window
A table with fruit and wine
Women in white dresses
Men smoking cigars
Near the porch young children capture moths
The dwindle of light
In the middle of the nineteenth century

Who knows how the man got through
What happened to the house and people
Darkness kept falling
Until nothing was left
Only the carriage
In the glow of fire after fire
Made a bee-line to the present
Along a road whose shoulders
Are bare with dying trees

Intersection

The golden height of summer
Hornets and bees
Play tag with the bullets of the past
Gendarmes from the partitions Cossacks
Members of the SS and common pedestrians
Skirt one another like the shadows of leaves
Falling from the branches of history

A Warsaw street basks in sunlight
People walk as if going to work
People headed for their death

This street leads nowhere
But to the end of all things
Barricades and dreams
Torn down
Only the smell of oblivion
Hangs in the air

Stone markers
Do not catch our eye
Only the pigeons
And red lights at the intersection
Of Asia and Europe

The Retreat of the Home Army*

Their resistance broken
Not by war
But from cancer
Or a heart by-pass

Those who survive
Are like gutted houses
Only memory
Left to glow in the ashes

Too late to build a fire
Too late to warm our hands

While from the murky heights
A glacier
Slides over Poland
Its red tongue

*The Home Army was the major armed resistance movement in Poland during World War II. Directed by the government-in- exile from London, after the war its members suffered persecution under the new government formed under the direction of Moscow.

The Flip Side of the Medal

Firing squads
Are made of flesh and blood
But their conscience
Is clammy

When the order is given
They close one eye
The other springs open
Like a wound

Each of us can stand
In the line of rifles
Or opposite
Our hands behind our backs

Yet Another Time

A white bird
In a small plastic cage
One wing lifted
It tries to fly

The city steps out from the shore of its streets
The tangled bodies of flowers
The sun smears sweat from the human fruit

Bird flower human we are all equal prey
To the stars and to the dust
Swirling in air

We want a miracle
But its rooms are all full
The grimy stairs and drunk janitor
A stripped bed and a woman
Who shakes her tablecloth out the window
The cry of a child and the draft
Slamming a door
On it the names of kings in crayon
This year long as the tail on a squirrel

And darkness fell in Judea
John in Herod's Castle
Sent out his disciples with these words of doubt
Are you the one who was prophesied
Or do we await another?

*Sleigh Ride**

My bearded driver has dozed. I pound on his back. Wake up,
you good for nothing! We'll get snowed in. We'll freeze. And he says:
I'm not sleeping, sir. I was only doing a bit of thinking. —About
what?—About you, sir. You're not Russian; you're not even from this
time. You got on the wrong sleigh, and now what are we to do? I can't
drive you to St. Petersburg, I can't drive you anywhere. You thought it
would be easy to whisk off on the memoirs of Herzen. But you
haven't got a prayer.
        And for emphasis he slaps his whip on the snowbank
hemming us in.

*Alexander Herzen (1812-1870), a prominent Russian social thinker in exile
from 1847 onward, edited the London-based journal *The Bells*, which, smuggled
back into his homeland, played an important role in nineteenth-century Russian
revolutionary thought. Herzen's influence on his countrymen, even amongst
fellow socialists, ended with his support of the Polish insurrection of 1863.

The Journey Forever

The stanzas roll by
Like the last cars of a rocking train
They disappear
In the undying throb of wheels

The straight lines stretch out
The wave of red and white semaphores
Unshaved brakemen and passengers who can't sleep

Past the wreckage of the Polish landscape
We travel from one station to the next
Smuggling our daily loaf of bread
The meat of our common tongue

*Exodus**

In a great hurried march
They came with their everyday belongings
Children dogs laundry
The quarrelling blue and white china
Mickiewicz dying of cholera
Bound in a gilded spine
Uprising crossed on top of uprising
And at last their common heart
An ailing muscle
Propped up on a dirty pillow
They fled to the year two thousand
Toward the snow-covered peaks
At the foot there had to be a trail

But they found no passage
Only one wall standing of a house
The gutted frame of a window
And it was then they saw

Their own backs were bent
Over the backs of other displaced people
And carried forth like a heavy cross

*Adam Mickiewicz died of cholera during a journey to Constantinople in order to aid Polish soldiers fighting against Russia in the Crimean War.

Prose (1989-1997)

Instruments of Crime

In 1984—not the book but the year—my typewriter was taken during a search of my apartment. But it didn't happen all at once. Later I even went to retrieve it from Rakowiecki Prison, where it was impounded because the fun-loving, blue-eyed captain in charge of the operation determined that since nothing of importance was found in the search, they must punish me for my perfidious caution by confiscating the tool of my trade. The typewriter was an old Continental, ancient but in perfect shape. I had received it from my father, Mieczslaw Jastrun, who among other things had written on it his book *Mickiewicz*, a part of the mandatory reading curriculum during high school. The officers who carried the typewriter away had no idea that they held in their hands the instrument responsible for their required reading once upon a time.

That same day I myself ended up being held for 48 hours in one of the dark and dank cells of the commissariat on Antoni Malczewski Street. Malczewski, alpinist and Romantic poet, on the peak of his wildest dreams would never have imagined that below his street, in such gloomy and smelly cellars, people would be locked up for writing poetry.

"I ran you in because you wrote a poem about me," my guardian angel at the commissariat had said cheerfully. And with these very words I started a new poem. Writing is such a terrible addiction.

Several months later, without a whole lot of hope, but rather with deep misgivings, I made my way back to Rakowiecki to take up the task again of reclaiming my typewriter. A well-padded officer in charge of complaints led me upstairs past some rooms I knew well, where on the walls the calendars with naked girls proclaimed that even here new times were on the horizon.

There was my typewriter sitting on a desk. Tenderly I stroked her sides . "No, not here," she warned. "Not in front of them." I had to write out an affidavit stating that the typewriter was in good condition and that I was here to claim it. Then, right in the doorway, I had a close encounter of the third kind with a short, elderly stubby-fingered man whom I already had the displeasure of meeting from time to time, and who gave himself out to be the head bookkeeper in charge of keeping track of the sins of the artistic world. Sneering at my haste to leave so quickly, he declared we needed to have a little chat in his office before the matter could be completely settled. He advised that I put the typewriter back on the desk and sit down and take a load off my feet. But when it appeared clear that only through the use of force would it be possible to seat me, he reflected for a moment and then said with total politeness, "We'll let you go ahead and stand."

110

I soon learned my poems were a bridgehead in the battle against the People's authority. And, moreover, an entire staff of specialists had proved that I had used this particular typewriter here to write three poems that had especially entrenched themselves in this bridgehead.

"We ask only one thing," the officer said, his short fingers clasped together on his belly, "that you give us some sort of affidavit—even an oral one would do"—he threw in amicably—"that you will not be writing any future work on this typewriter that would besmudge People's Poland." I stood there in silence, not, however, avoiding staring back as he stared at me. After several minutes of this exchange, which seemed like a veritable war of faces from a Gombrowicz novel, he finally cried out, "Why are you looking at me like that? I bet you're thinking that soon the tables will be turned, but, no way, no way will that ever be!" It's curious what swirls in some people's heads on the nights they can't get to sleep.

My further silence must have been taken for a sign of insolent rebellion, because then I heard that action was indeed going to be taken against me—of course a patent fiction because my case would be covered by the approaching amnesty anyway—but the typewriter itself would still be forfeited as an instrument of crime.

"We are letting you go this time only because we know your family is expecting you." Then he tore to his feet, which gave me the impression he had just been jerked by a leash. I left without the typewriter and without the affidavit that I was reclaiming it. The only thing I had was a feeling of being covered with lice. Soon afterwards I received word that my typewriter was still under investigation.

Unfortunately, the investigation of the typewriter is still going on. Surely it doesn't have much left it would want to confess. In such a situation I can only admit further that I have a second typewriter at home and that on it I have written other texts that make up the remainder of the bridgehead against People's Poland. The officers carrying out yet another search of my home even saw it, though this time they didn't take this dangerous instrument, I suspect because it wasn't just a matter of the machine being dangerous, not just that at all. Rather, they came just because they wanted to show us again that our apartment doesn't have doors, that laws can be broken in the blink of another law, that words can be shut inside a jail.

In the margin, I would also like to establish that there had also been left in Solidarity's Mazowsze Region Headquarters (where I worked and which had been overrun by the authorities at the start of martial law), a Christmas package for our son, that my wife had left an umbrella and a wicker basket, and that I had left behind a rather handy space heater with a ventilator fan. I'm sorry that in such public times I write about private matters. Still, these private concerns have a more general dimension at the moment. The time has perhaps come for the office of confiscated articles to be converted to an equipment rental agency.—*Gazeta Wyborcza, No. 34, June 23-25, 1989.*

/ 111

Audience

The first day after the holidays I have a meeting with the Minister of Internal Affairs, Czeslaw Kiszcak. It's with great ceremony that the Great Office is finally returning to me what they confiscated back in 1984—a typewriter, a batch of books, and some manuscripts.

Over the phone I give the license plate number to my tiny Fiat, and then I must decide and tell them whether I will drive in from Rakowiecka Street or from the direction of the SuperSam Grocery Store. I savor this dilemma like the very aroma of freedom. Rakowiecka is my obvious choice, but unfortunately they've redone the entrance, so I won't be able enter through the same narrow passage that so ceremoniously a while back swallowed up a white Polonez—with me in it, wearing the handcuffs so fashionable at the time. It was a gloomy November afternoon in 1982. How peculiar the city looked from behind that windowglass. People on the street walked along so slowly, as if dragging their feet about something they needed to do, as if idiotically removed from the glaring fact that they were free.

My typewriter wasn't taken until after a search of my home in 1984, meaning that for several years I had been able to get away scot free with pursuing my sinister conspiracies against the state on its keyboard. But finally it was confiscated—as if their waking me at 6 a.m. wasn't cruelty enough. During a search of my apartment they had found nothing, and so they later made yet another trip back from Rakowiecka just to fetch the typewriter.

Right now, driving along Rakowiecka with a much lighter heart, the wind hits me in the face, and with it the bits and pieces of secret police voices from all through the years:

"Your father is dying, and it is because of you he is dying, your activities in the underground."

"In comparison to the poem of H, yours is second-rate. We can prove it."

"The investigation we're conducting is actually a fake."

"I'm getting out of the car. I'm going to pray for you in that little church there" (on the way to Bialoleka, in a spot disarmingly close to an apartment where I had stashed evidence of great relevance to my case).

"In the morning, we'll start from scratch" (very unpleasant words after an all-night interrogation).

And the finest conversation of all, a fifteen minute silent exchange of dour looks, a battle of Gombrowicz-like faces, with a certain colonel, the chief of the department for Artistic Affairs. And then his final outburst: "Why are you looking at me like that? Do you think we are going to be trading places?" (And how bizarre, that the secret police officer's nightmare has become flesh, that soon I could knock this certain colonel off his stool right here in this very same department.)

But suddenly I feel shame, that the bits and pieces I mention here, my own paltry "martyrology," could be considered as boasting. I think of the doleful struggles that others have had (especially given the situation with today's increasingly decomposing "spirit of compromise"), or the fates of those who have to do truly serious jail time. My scrapes with the secret police were not some overwhelming torture. Nevertheless, revulsion remains: my life for an entire year having to be spent outside of my own home, and a life spent even longer afterwards living in a house with no real doors, the feelings of weakness and shattered nerves.

I've sketched this modest little chapter of mine from Rakowiecka in order to convey the lightness that walked arm in arm with me as I disappeared into the north wing of the building, where the Minister himself resides. In this part of the Ministry, the corridors are as empty as if Kafka is dreaming the whole thing. Only somewhere further, on one of the higher floors, sits a man in uniform—though who can tell if real or made of wax? I'm worried I'll be lost for good in this farflung, sterile maze. But eventually I reach the final floor, where a policeman swoops out of nowhere like a blue ghost and mentions politely that if I wish I may hang up my coat. As I do so, I instinctively remove my wallet and slide it into my back pocket. A nice-looking young secretary, and nearby, a nice-looking young guard, both smile and look delighted. I knock politely on the door, reinforcing the absurdity of such conventional behavior, since the doors are reinforced with steel. And then, on the other side of the door, already stands the General, smiling, looking delighted also. The office is unusually spacious. I gauge with my eye whether it could be turned into an indoor tennis court. On the very spacious table is my typewriter. Nearby is a folder of typewritten manuscripts. Then, for a moment, the general is flustered. He doesn't know whether to lead me to the typewriter or to the table for visitors. Indeed, how can one, in the same moment, both restore what was seized and at the same time ask the injured party to have a little chit-chat? Eventually we sit down, however, and a pretty young woman brings us in tea with lemon. Looking around, I feel a certain agitation; right here in this room decisions were made that would change my entire life, that broke the bones of this country, which today still remain in a cast.

So, now, with an uncommon twist of fate, I clamber up onto the summit of Martial Law, in order to take a seat on its four-cornered peak (still capable of pricking our backsides) with one of the head architects of this structure that already has turned into a relic, covered with the moss of time. What can be seen from such a place? Dregs and confusion, for the most part. Smoke, dust, and cloud.

The general recounts how in the day before Zero Hour he flipped through a list of people to be interned, marking out a few, but didn't catch the name of Professor Klemens Szaniawski. An idiotic affair, since just the day before he had been with Szaniawski and Gieysztor, drinking cognac.

How everything runs together, I think. The overlooking of one professor in a forest of ten thousand names, of people whose doors were later broken down, sends shivers down my spine. Because, on that same unforgettable night (having missed the four operatives on their way to my house with a crowbar), I ended up visiting station after station, not so much of the Divine Passion, but of the Grotesque—and ended up at the tower beside the church of St. Anne, where with difficulty I managed to wake up Father N. The Father was quite upset, and asked if he needed to put on his cassock. Then, he in his cassock and I without one, headed off into the peaceful, fluffy snow to the nearby rectory, where we had to pound with all our four fists to wake up the parish priest from his sleep. (Right then I had the naive notion it was absolutely necessary to wake up and inform even the Primate, when, actually, it was God himself that needed raising on that night.) The parish priest was visibly unhappy that we were keeping him from his rest, especially since fifteen minutes before he had been disturbed by some young people bearing the news that Professor Szaniawski had been arrested. "His wife would not let go, so they arrested her, too," the priest said offhandedly, yawning. I felt a cold shiver run up and down my back. If they can lock up a mild-mannered professor along with his wife, then that means we must be in Cambodia already.

I left the rectory bedroom—sent off with the priest's sign of the cross made so painstakingly I could feel its weight upon my back; and, once out on the street, I glimpsed how painful it was to feel completely without hope. On this night I saw too many homes without doors, or too many homes that did have doors, hiding people lost in the weight of sleep, grasping onto their nightshirts and pajamas over their soft, oh so soft, bellies. Then there was "The Wedding," at my friends' home, where drunken couples danced, not listening to my pleas. Then, feeling betrayed by both friend and priest, I decided to approach the people of Warsaw themselves, and so I drove to a nearby taxistand, where in the shadow of the Zygmunt Column a sizable crowd was standing. I jumped out of my car and launched into some kind of insurrectionary speech. The crowd, visibly stirred, poured towards me, but without warning I was suddenly assaulted with all manner of alcohol fumes. I fled in panic back inside the car and took off, my wheels spinning in the deep snow. The drunks plastered themselves all over the vehicle, their faces on the front windshield, on the side, the back, their hands like slimy tentacles. Then I picked up speed, and they fell off behind me like leeches.

114

And then afterwards—that year of Martial Law and the delights of conspiracy. (We should put the word conspiracy in quotation marks, or on one side at least.)

The memories dance on in irony—I'd even stake my life on it—yes, in irony, right here on the swaying surface of the tea we pour down our gullets, in accord and harmony, the Minister and I.

It would be naive to get into an argument with the architect of Martial Law over how sensible he had been. And frightening. For should I convince him, the General would have to commit suicide, and if he convinced me, I would have to commit something as well. So I avoid posing the question in this manner, but still there is no avoiding his assertion that "otherwise the Russians would have come in, and the pressures after the imposition of 'the war' would have been greater from both inside and out." The Minister lets it be known that we could not imagine how difficult the decision had been to make. Curious, I think, how everyone suffered back then, and then I think also that even if what he says is the truth, this truth does not equal a true justification. By way of particulars, I have questions as to how the decision was made to employ that cunning little military tactic of playing over the radio the tapes of bugged telephone calls, not to mention the conversation between Lech Walesa and his brother that wasn't even over the phone. Only superficially do such maneuvers seem more innocent than out and out torture, because in reality any government capable of such action is in fact saying to its subjects: "To anyone who's not behaving we can give a public enema—and even take away their life like it was meat from a dog."

The Minister anguished over such governmental surveillance of individuals. But, courageously, he still took responsibility for doing that awful thing upon himself. At the time he wasn't doing so well, he had to get some rest, he delegated some of the decision-making to others, and, besides, there was a constant stream of "Here's material on this. Here's material on that." He went off to take a nap so as not to completely fall asleep through the next couple of nights. And it happened. But, still, he admits, the buck stops with him. Beautiful, no?

To the end of our conversation I conduct myself beautifully as well, for I have the gall to say they have returned my typewriter and the rest of the confiscated items as if out of favoritism, not on the foundation of some permanent law. Indeed, there were thousands of others who had even more taken away and who have received neither restoration nor compensation. I may hear of the Ministry's good intentions now, but a large measure of these items were given away into divers hands a long time ago. And so how to get them back? "The law was like it was, but it was the law," the Minister declares.

I had hoped that when I came out of the lion's den, besides my typewriter I could carry out some momento, even if just one rotten tooth. But I left only with the typewriter: there are just no teeth left.

—*September 1990*

from *Exterior Journal*

. . .Warsaw's International Book Fair had traditionally been held in The Palace of Culture so now, making themselves at home here in the belly of Stalin's gift to the Polish people, were books from the underground press as well as several emigré publishing houses— none of which was I able to reach, by the way, lost as I was in the labyrinth of bookstalls. The swirl of people in front of these alternative press stalls was indescribable, all the more so because to a large degree the crowds were all made up of people who know each other, and it's common knowledge that there is no larger throng of people than one's acquaintances stuffed to bursting with mutual remembrances, with common likes and dislikes. The heads of the independent publishing houses as well as their assistants and their assistants' assistants all sat around flustered, their eyes squinting like underground moles which have suddenly found themselves out in the glare of the sun. I found out from them that during the morning various dignitaries had made an appearance to (in a way) bless the place. And thus what was the day before yesterday totally illegal and yesterday quasi-illegal was today totally above board. And to think that it all happened within the framework of the very same laws. Law to us is like chewing gun, everything depends on who puts it in their mouth and what shape they mold it into later on. With great emotion I looked over all the book covers roosting there on the shelves of the stalls, so meager and weary, like birds whose wing-feathers have faded in the course of a long flight, filled with high wind and thunderstorm. And not everything was able to fly in all the way. Then, suddenly, I was face to face with my own name on several of the covers. It was as if I had just spied my own snout—no, not my face, my snout—in the mirror unexpectedly. Was this some sort of negative reaction to what had been written, to myself; or, to that former time—whose sense of heroism kept melting away year after year until at some point it just turned into a dung heap? The Round Table changed all of that to a big cauldron of vegetable soup, and it will be interesting as hell to see what else comes bubbling out.

It was then I head a boisterous greeting and a hand stuck out in my direction. I shook it just like the hand of someone I knew I knew but couldn't quite place exactly. Since I do in fact possess a bad memory for faces, I have developed a rather elaborate strategy for handling such situations: I let on I know the person, while awaiting further developments in the hope I will receive just the right data to unravel my puzzle. But this time almost immediately I felt an unease, the source of which was both the guy's out-of-touch necktie and the suspicious color of his suit.

—You don't recognize your own oppressor?

It wasn't the word oppressor that put me on the scent. Rather, it was the slight wafting of a lisp which years before had streamed toward me through a whole day and night and clear until the next white of day. It was right after I had been apprehended during martial law. During that twenty-four hour interrogation on Rakowiecka this lisp had slowly pasted itself to every object in the room until it had ensconced itself inside my head, and for a long time afterwards I couldn't wash it out, sitting there as I was in the Bialoleka "boarding house."

—Captain? Sir?

—Please don't demote me, I beg of you.

It's an interesting country. Everyone got promoted equally, both those who lost and those who won. But, who actually has won? Rather, did everyone just lose?

Despite the fact I could engage in such convoluted thoughts, I was so completely flustered by this meeting as well as so totally unprepared to deal with him that out of pure reflex I drew my torturer off to the side where, to stand with someone like him in the midst of all these former underground publishers, seemed to be truly preposterous.

—Are you here on business?

—It's hard to say. They assigned me to books. We've sure waded right into this culture business with our boots on.

And with dirty boots at that, I should have said, but didn't, because all sorts of thoughts were sliming up my mind, which already was uncertain as to whether everything here was really happening or not.

Then a woman friend of mine whom I had not seen for ages, an amazing beauty indeed, ran right up to me and kissed me, then plop immediately goes and extends her hand out to the Major. I lunged forward in order to stop her hand before its virtue became compromised. But I was too late, and I just waved the whole situation off with my own hand, as if I was chasing off a ghost.

And so the ghost went away, with a painful look on his face. Always they have envied us our women, our dollars, our trips out of the country and that which they themselves always scornfully call our "moral luxury."

So why did he buttonhole me in such an extraordinary place? It was like a mouse in amongst the cats. All I had to do was grab him by the tail of his necktie and raise a ruckus. Look sharp o independent torch of enlightenment! Here's a moth drawn to the flame though it will mean his death!

Please don't be afraid. For a long time now I've not troubled my brain over the complexities of a secret policeman's soul. I know there is nothing there worth noticing. The only problem that seems interesting is that of victim and victimizer, and the flow of time. Why is it that people tortured during the course of an investigation almost never seek retaliation years later? (I personally never suffered any cruel violation from the Major, though he still richly deserves the loss of his teeth.) This isn't just a diluting over time of suffering wrongs; they will live with us to the end of our days. And hatred—its muscles may get flabby, but it still will not die. But rage from that former time always feels rather obsessive, towards that long ago torturer. That's why revenge is always so paltry, because it's always carried out by someone other than the victim on somebody other than the original victimizer so that the strife just doubles.

After a few days of constantly returning in my mind to that meeting, I realized that even in the first shock of the surprise there had been something that had hidden itself deep in my brain. His hands. His entire hands shook like two helpless aspen leaves, disturbed by an unseen breeze. . . .—*Kultura (Paris), November 1989*

from *Awry*

August 1990

Okecie. The word entangled inside of itself like a bunch of roots. Okecie where there occurred so many greetings and farewells that over the years they meshed together into a single fabric in the shape of an old felt slipper. Okecie, full of police gauntlets and horrific document checks, of customs officials with noses molded out of asphalt. And the border, which bares its fangs as someone nears. It's at that point that our own hearts contract like the hearts of rabbits, and even Poles living in the West suffer from this spasm when they cross this barely non-existent boundary-—when after ten years of living in the free world this syndrome for the most part has disappeared. And during martial law those very extraordinary emigration flights out of the country of those close to us, the blast from the jet engines carrying the smell of fuel, which at the time seemed to be the gust of wind from a freedom inaccessible to us.

Today Okecie has wasted away; the border fear has flagged. Because the border has now only become the boundary between our own impotence—our own garbage pile—and that other world. Only that former heart spasm remains. With therapeutic treatment, will our hearts last another ten years?

I'm looking for some customs officials, but I don't see any. Only some young women are scurrying about, probably custom officers in training. They seem lost inside this multi-story mess. They ask if I am here for customs inspection, while I respond that I'm above inspection. They're a little astonished, but not a lot, and just smile at me helplessly.

Today Okecie is above all an indescribable throng, a mob pushing its way onto Noah's Ark. And if it is a flood everyone flees, then it's a flood of freedom, whose waters carry with them who knows what. My eyes then catch sight of the head of Magister De Virion towering over the crowd. He too seems all in a flutter, fleeing off to London in order to take over control of the Polish Embassy. We thus escape from the overflow of freedom in many different ways, even through diplomatic posts.

We are fleeing Poland itself, a Poland which is free, but which we just cannot lift, and the problem isn't that it's heavy, but that we just can't get a handhold. Two hundred years shattered with a hammer, smothered fifty years or so by the Soviet system (in order to use their hands, they had to sit on our faces with their butts), we've lost our shape entirely. And we ourselves don't know if we are some proud nobility or just a bunch of smalltime Jewish merchants driven away from the market stalls of Europe. And our patriotism, our national symbols, our many famous virtues, where are they?

Lately I have moved about in Poland with increasingly greater difficulty, as if something were hindering my movements. And I started falling into the state that a certain writer has termed "absolute impotence." Because standing here in front of our parched lips is a glass of bottled spring water with the label of Europe on it. We reach out our hand, and this hand has no fingers, it's only a stump. Thus, never before was Europe so close and yet so far. Impotence on each step of our ladder, if there are any steps at all.

We aren't even able to manage the money that the West throws us from time to time, the problem of course being that after such bad experiences it won't ever throw the dog a scrap again. The dog just wolfed everything down—one, two, three—and everything was for naught. Now, the West requires a precise plan as to what we intend to do with that money. And there the problems begin.

Numerous businessmen still fly into Poland, counting on making deals. They fly out, strangely flustered and distressed. M. is a businessman of Polish descent, so isn't arriving in Poland as if to an alien planet full of strange, stupefying phenomena. Still, he relates that never before has he ever found it so difficult to arrange anything at all. Some people got lost inside all the changing regulations, and some people often got lost there intentionally. Government officials waiting for the axe to fall on their jobs often hide from execution in the thicket of paragraphs and rules, sporting this same-as-always hungered expression on their faces as they state, "This matter cannot be arranged." But a well-practiced eye will glimpse in these words a tiny crack through which can always squeeze the fingers of a third hand—that devil's appendage from socialism—that hand holding a bribe.

Yesterday a conversation with S. He just got back from "Poland," quite downcast, he says, so much so it was the last transport he'll ever make. He's had enough. For years S. has carried medical equipment into Poland, which he himself bought. Now he just got through standing on the border two days in a big fat vehicular tail. The second day this tail started to impart from itself a rotting smell, due to the decay of citrus fruits thousands of tradesmen were trying to bring in to the country. . . .—*Kultura (Paris), September 1990*

November 1990

. . . In the entrance to a building where some friends live is a sign which was not there a little while ago: Weapons and Ammunition Sold Here. I think they used to sell sofa-beds in this place. Then by the door to my friends' apartment I was disturbed by a mechanism that hardly looked to be humanitarian. Later I found out it was an alarm. My friends had decided to install it after a certain evening when they happened, of all things, to be watching a crime movie on tv when they heard their doorbell ring. They decided not to open up, even though the person kept ringing. Then suddenly the door gave way and there appeared the shiny little snout of a crowbar.

After such an adventure they put up the alarm, about which they're apprehensive as well. And, worst of all, they still don't know if it's better to open the door or not open the door whenever someone starts ringing.

The majority of buildings in our cities now feature intercoms to get into the building. Many boast the luxuriant whiskers of satellite antennas. We enter Europe spastically, as if crawling along on all fours. Plus, it seems like we come in through the basement. Right now, that's all the farther we have gone.

I meet up with K. As usual, he's on the run, and, as always, he seems on the verge of a heart attack. What's new? Of course he complains about the lack of time. Yesterday of course we had all sorts of time. It was one of the attractions of living there in the absurdity of socialism. Now in Poland time is like having diarrhea. Not much will come of it, but everyone's still on the run. . .

A huge crowd in the cemeteries. The Day of the Dead is obviously a holiday for the living. It's the sad jubilation from those still living for those who are no more. Walking through Powazki Cemetery I had the feeling I was at an extraordinary gathering. So many acquaintances, often in the highest seats of power. Here Minister X rubs his hand around in mine, we say nothing, but I know the message—he's having a very hard time. And there film director Andrzej Wajda jangles a collection box for grave renovation. Powazki indeed gets prettier and prettier, though the newer sections of our cities may be changing to ruins. Shaking hands, I thread my way through the crowd. Right now I'm by the grave of the poet Lesmian, who already had dematerialized so much during life that it's easy to imagine his real self being here. Then S. runs into me. What's going on with publishers? —Awful. It seems that no one wants to stay alive anymore .

I recall that during martial law, already beyond hope, I'd walked around in this cemetery. Here I felt better than I did anywhere else, more certain, secretly envious of those lying here underneath their stone quilts. Then the wheel of history turned and we were on top, though it's not very comfortable where we are now, either.

A packed bus takes me downtown. S. spies me and yells through the sea of heads. —I'm voting for Mazowiecki, but our editorial staff has split in half on the matter. In general we're just wasting away as a magazine.

I leave the bus in front of The Palace of Culture with relief: I have the feeling S. has told me more than I wanted to know. In the October chill The Palace of Culture looks like a splinter of carved ice, and the statues of workers and great Poles holding up the bottom of the monolith all have expressions of unspeakable suffering. The wind careens all over the great square, pausing for a moment near a small group of people. Street merchants. In a normal day there would be bubbling here what is probably the largest open air market in Europe. But on a day like this who would muster up the courage?

Soviet tourists. Their faces more batted about by history than ours are. Is there anything these Soviet peoples wouldn't have for sale, only yesterday the inhabitants of Heaven on Earth? Screwdrivers, binoculars, caviar. But, the little samovar is not for sale. There must be tea to warm up! From out of the pocket of this one little guy pokes a small icon as if it just happened to be perching there by accident. Some Romanians have spread themselves out on the ground. They're not selling anything. They sit there, holding up tattered cards that say, "We are homeless Romanians. Help us!" Tiny children circle in and around them like small animals with prehensile limbs. The square looks like a single branch of a great refuge camp from the disintegrating Eastern Europe, a giant war-time market. And in the background the wide hips of The Palace of Culture, which is probably going to be bought by an American billionaire. I'm curious as to who will buy poor Lenin right out from his Kremlin mausoleum, and for how much. . . .—*Kultura (Paris), Decembeer 1990*

April 1991

. . . A meeting of a group of intellectuals from Eastern Europe. Serb, Hungarian, Slovenian, Estonian, Romanian. Russians. Our eastern arithmetic of freedom—helplessness and despair—added, multiplied, divided. In the best shape are the Russians. They get drunk and of course start singing, puffing themselves up like overstuffed balloons, revealing an infrastructure of gold and silver teeth. But there in their baritones no longer appears the might of empire--just dancing hippos in a circus. I don't know what to think. I mix compassion and liking with scorn, at which this drink we're drinking goes down particularly hard. I clink shot glasses with the Slovenians. They seem to be drinking the same way. They are probably the most European of all our gathering. . . .—*Kultura (Paris), May 1991*

February 1992

My generation is caught up in that awkward stage where there's a gray line running between young middle age and being truly old. It's a boundary of several years, and if through this time people don't run into each other regularly then they are always in for a shock when they do. It's the most compelling—and public—drama around, against which any particular political spectacle doesn't stand a chance. Women wilt as if they were flowers cut short by an early winter. Men suddenly grow bellies; earlier there may have been indications of an

122

inclination towards this, but for the most part these earlier examples were just temporary bellies, almost like people sub-letting an apartment. Now, they have made themselves at home permanently, and are carried around without shame as if a natural part of the scenery. Among the violent changes is the way the subject of men's conversations have altered as well. Once the talk mainly involved politics and outcries against communism, whereas now the decided majority of conversations revolve around money or business. During Poland's socialist period, time was one thing of which there never was a shortage. And precisely on top of this one good was built a number of pleasant things. Only now do we realize the loss of such amenities, and that we didn't realize how good we had it, though that good took place inside a greater evil.

This keeping at a hectic pace is a sickness in the entire Western civilized world. Already, we're not running around any less than they are, but here it's problematic that all this commotion is taking place in ultra-unsanitary conditions, while it's also unknown whether we're busy building up or tearing down. And it's all at fever pitch—because there isn't any time, because at any moment all hell will break loose, so everyone needs to count the money quickly and then head for the bushes.

It strikes me that everyone is opening up a company. Almost to a person, practically everyone I know has founded something, so much so that I feel like a complete idiot without a firm of my own. And it's all taking place in a situation in which only for a moment does the gold vein of commerce glitter. Already the situation's back to not being profitable again. And I've never been able to discover what all these companies do anyway. From various murmurs and mumblings I've gathered that they bring in goods and transfer them around. No one produces anything. It's as if the factories don't even produce. There's something here I'm just not getting. Are all these storefronts currently ablaze with trade all obtaining their building materials from our basements and foundations? And what will happen, if they pull out too much.

I get together with a doctor, a friend from the old days. He lives in a small town a hundred kilometers from the capital. He is a doctor by calling. He specifically moved out to the provinces, and it wasn't for money. It was a mission. I remember he was greatly loved and esteemed in the town and in the neighboring villages.

—What's new with you? I ask him, certain that he at least—our modern Doctor Schweister—would not just start in complaining.

He gives me a business card, which already is enough to disturb me. A business card from his pocket is an alien thing. Then I read. There on the card is his name and the following advertisement: "The latest methods in hair restoration." He no longer works in a hospital and doesn't hide the fact that he's now a millionaire. Even in the village there are peasants who would give a pretty penny to get back their lost hair.

—Such are the times, he says, heaving a sigh.—*Kultura (Paris), March 1992*

June 1997

In the Royal Castle a meeting between Szymborska and Milosz, between Milosz and Szymborska. Everyone has predicted it will be a huge event indeed, because the two greatest Polish artistic successes of the second half of the century will be conversing with each other. But before the meeting a few individuals close to the Nobel Laureates still had certain apprehensions, stemming from the fact that Szymborska does not like to speak in public and in fact feels most at ease when she can publically keep quiet. Milosz on the other hand, who likes to speak in public and is in great shape in this regard, does not hear the best, which of course does not discourage monologue, but does impair dialogue. But the ominous portents were shrugged off, and the room awash in mirrors and gold was filled with the Polish elite, now awaiting history to take place.

The Laureates appeared with an entourage—a much too numerous entourrage—of photojournalists. A woman's choir dressed in green robes intoned a song in Latin. Meanwhile, the Laureates were positioned opposite two chairs and then offered as prey to the photographers. In the midst of the countless flashes, in the angelic singing, the two appeared to be heaven's elect. Szymborska was suffering, wishing she could dematerialize on the spot, while Milosz scowled with dignity. This scene lasted so frightfully long as to tax even the strongest constituion, but the Laureates survived this trial of the flash and, once more elevated on the wings of the choir, they neared the antique table swarming with microphones. The tops of the microphones looked like the heads of snakes. Two chairs courteously awaited. But thereupon arose a problem. Who would sit on which side? "So you here and I there. No, I here and you there. I there, you here. . ." From such a dialogue, I realized, would arise a poem not so much in the style of Milosz or Szymborska, but rather like Bialoszewski. And so the two Laureates tripped over each other's feet—here, no there—not able to make a decision. Then finally Milosz's cane decided and fell down to the floor.

Next the microphones revealed their venom. They didn't work. Milosz couldn't hear, and the two moderators plunged deeper and deeper into hopelessness and despair. But why? These were the best silent film gags I had seen in years.

I cannot attest that, in the fragments able to be heard, there did not fall any valuable words, or even phrases essential for our culture. But, I do not remember any. Rather, I remember how Szymborska suddenly grew silent and looked around as if she had just lost her purse, then saying in desperation that she had "lost the thread." In the room was a general stir, but no one found the thread that was lost. Maybe no one dared return it. Maybe someone kept it as a souvenir.

"Such a lack of professionalism," Janusz Glowacki, fresh off the plane from New York, said to me later. And, I responded: "Thank goodness. How boring it would be there in your New York, while here we had fun like crazy."

For the finale they held a reception, where a waiter with a humongous knife cut something my empty stomach recognized to be a giant cake, but which turned out unfortunately to be only a giant sandwich the size of a small sofa. And suddenly I had the most horrible thought. What if the waiter with the big knife would suddenly tear into our Nobel Laureates and deprive them of life? He would enter literary history, whereas none of the hundreds of uncommonly worthy guests at this most exclusive debate would ever make it there.

In the glow of this meeting I return home, where before my building the mafia from my neighborhood is basking in the sun, in the fellowship of the local drunks who, in their moments of relative sobriety, provide the mafia with various services.

The mafia guys hang out by their limos, yelling and cutting up. They are quite sure of themselves, and quite happy with life. They hold court right across from the Internal Affairs Building, where once I was hauled in in handcuffs. Currently the workers in this fortress are my allies, but I don't have the slightest impression that they would ever attempt to corral the mafia. Right then my neighbor joins the group, drunk as a skunk. For years he's been dying from cancer, and for years he been after me, since I'm a writer, to do a book on his dying. But how to explain to him nicely that everyone sooner or later will have to undergo their own dying? I realize that in this moment his own death is the most important one, but if a book were to be made from every death, the whole world would die from the glut of bad books on the process of dying. . . .—*Kultura (Paris), July/August 1997*

Late Spring 1997

I get into the #2 tram at my stop at the intersection of Pulawska and Marszalkowska. At this crossroads, a huge bank is rising up at an unbelievable pace, right next to the hole where the Moscow Movie Theater once stood. The building that was supposed to be erected here was touted as a cultural center, but that was just a camouflage for the building of this commercial behemoth. I found about all this from some people at City Hall who were both outraged and bitter. But, why did they keep silent? That cultural center will not get erected. Not enough money, but also not enough of something else as well. There is no movie theater here. There is a hole.

Then in the tram I witnessed a cartoonish scene, but one which speaks much in regards to various Polish traits-—already waning perhaps, though still in existence. Barreling into the tram was a fellow in horrific shape. He was drunk, crazy and aggressive. He flung himself around in the car, spit and curses foaming from his mouth. I was aware of having a great desire to bash the guy's brains in, but I also knew that if I hit him very hard at all my arm would go into the swamp of his brain all the way up to the elbow. But then the guy crashed on his own into a seat and started howling. The area around him quickly emptied. Then when the tramway stopped again, an elderly woman got on. The drunk instantly tore himself up on shaky legs, with great difficulty regaining his balance, and then with a wide open gesture pointed to the empty chair. The woman thanked him and sat down. Meanwhile, above her the drunk rocked back and forth. It was evident he was getting sick to his stomach, but that he was trying to hold it all in. Then he staggered off down to the other end of the car, where he stood over another old lady and looked down at her with his totally bloodshot eyes. The woman showed herself to be incredibly nimble in leaving her seat while the drunk crashed down on the chair like a sack of potatoes. Then the drunk went quiet and still, evidently satisfied with himself.

This is how deep and twisted are the roots of certain of our noble impulses. But all that is now ending, burning out, transforming. And great is the mixture within us of something rotten as well as something new, youthful, beautiful. But what will be the proportions? And what will it all add up to?—*Kultura (Paris), June 1997*

Acknowledgements

Abraxas: "The Fall," "Him" and Shipwreck"

Another Chicago Magazine: "Echoes" and "Prison"

Antigonish Review: "Five Before Twelve," "Ground Cover," and "Yet Another Time"

Artful Dodge: "Beasts" and "Chasm"

Beloit Poetry Journal: "Guardian Angel" and "The Last Days of My Guardian Angel"

Chariton Review: "City" and "Freedom"

Chelsea: "Eyes," "Fruitless," "Gotland," "Lights," "Nothing," and "Underneath This Leaf"

Colorado Review: "Each Night" and "Straw"

Colorado North Review: "Eyebrows," "Uncertain Ground," and "Vacation"

Confrontation: "Alms," "Monuments," and "Sleeplessness"

Connecticut Poetry Review: "Our Table of Desire" and "Peasant Farmer"

Cumberland Poetry Review: "In a Cage" and "Zomo"

Cutbank: "The Detention Camp"

Graham House Review: "The Flip Side of the Medal" and "The Retreat of the Home Army"

Greenfield Review: "Hat," "Interrogation with Map," "Prose," "Reunion," "Rings," "Tread," and "Visiting Day"

Literary Review: "Fatherland" and "Silence"

Mid-American Review: "Coming To," "Defeat," "In the Exercise Yard," and "In Mourning (1983)"

Minnesota Review: "A Call for Peace"

Mississippi Valley Review: "Babel," "Removing a Rich Farmer," "The Rose," "Seed" and "Single File"

Mr. Cogito: "Early in the Day," "In the Kitchen," "Live Shells," "Our Children of the Emigration," "Our Lady of Helplessness," "Paying a Visit," and "Road"

New Orleans Review: "Stony Brook on Long Island"

Northwest Review: "Board," "The First Night," "Forty Eight Hours,""Interrogation with Map," "Leaving Prison," "Light," "On the Crossroads," "Our Grammar," "Scrap," "Small Fires," "To My Son," and "Windows"

Ohio Review: "The Great Emigration"

Partisan Review: "Visitation"

Poet Lore: "Fog"

Poetry East: "Alarm," "Hands," "Instruments of Torture," "Planet," "Rat," and "Small Grains"

Prairie Schooner: "Elevator" and "Feathers"

Quarterly West: "Five Year Plan," "The Journey Forever," "Preparing for Bed," "A School in No One's Name," and " Sleigh Ride"
River Styx: "Leaving the House" and "The Year 1864"
Salmagundi: "Milk" and "A Secret Meeting"
Shenandoah: "A Letter from Prison"
South Carolina Review: "Possessed"
Visions: "Children and Soldiers" and "Pulp"
Webster Review: "Afghanistan" and "Polish Dogs"
Willow Springs: "Exodus," "Father and Son," and "Our Black Madonna of Czestochowa"
Witness: "Intersection" and "Tending One's Garden"
Xanadu: "The Cry"

Several of the poems above also appeared in various anthologies. "The Hat" and "Scrap" in *Child of Europe* (Penguin), ed. Michael March, and also in *Against Forgetting: Twentieth Century Poetry of Witness* (Norton), ed. Carolyn Forché. "Father and Son" in *This Same Sky* (Four Winds Press/MacMillan), ed. Naomi Shihab Nye. "Small Grains" in *The Last Believer in Prose* (Poetry East), ed. Richard Jones. "The Captive Dream" "Chasm," "Fatherland," "Prose," and "Silence" in *Shifting Borders: East European Poetries of the Eighties* (Associated University Presses, ed. Walter Cummins).

Thanks especially to Tomasz Jastrun, who not only lived and wrote these poems, but also provided patient illumination of various passages that aided tremendously during their journey into English. Also, to Karen Kovacik, whose help in selecting the translations and eagle eye in helping to hone them was irreplacable. Also, to John E. Smelcer and Leonard Kress for their careful feedback on the final manuscript as well as to Margaret Meeker Bourne, Timothy Wiles, Mary McGann, Alexander Fiut, Samuel Fiszman, Holly Kyle, Michael Hahn, Daniel Darling, Mieczyslaw Orksi, Krystyna Salitra, Ryszard Holzer, Irena Kiedrowska, Karen Ledwin, Piotr Sommer, Tonya and Donnie Hundley, Jan Kubik, and Urszula Tempska, all of whom helped in bringing translator and poet together or the poems from Polish into English. I am grateful too for the support I've received from the College of Wooster (including the Henry Luce III Fund for Distinguished Scholarship), the Polish Studies Center at Indiana University, the American Studies Center at Warsaw University, the Fulbright program, the Slavic and East European Library at the University of Illinois, and the Lilly Library of Indiana University.